STOCKS FOR BEGINNERS

THE BEGINNER'S GUIDE TO SUCCESSFULLY NAVIGATING THE STOCK MARKET, GROWING YOUR WEALTH & CREATING A SECURE FINANCIAL FUTURE

ROBERT EATON

COPYRIGHT

CONTENTS

INTRODUCTION

There is a very good reason why, to many, investing in stocks is regarded as the holy grail of passive income; when wisely chosen, they allow you to earn money while you sleep.

With a little bit of guidance, anyone can become a successful trader or investor; it is simply a matter of preparation.

If you are a rookie thinking of diving into the stock market, then consider this book your first investment.

This is your crash course on the basics of trading and investing. You won't find complicated strategies or schemes here. Before any of that, you need to lay a solid foundation, which is exactly what this book will help you achieve.

Before you place any money in the markets you owe it to yourself to understand what you are getting into. This book will teach you, step-by-step, the absolute essentials.

By the time you have finished reading, you will be ready to decide which road to go down and, under my professional guidance, I'll get you heading straight for success!

INTRODUCTION

So, let's get started.

STOCKS 101: THE BASICS

You may have heard people babbling into their cell phone, furiously ordering someone on the other end to "shift $1,000 of Facebook stock" or "buy 100 shares in the oil company", but what does it all mean?

Simply put, it means that person owns or wants to purchase a piece of a particular company. In essence, a stock is a part ownership of a publicly listed company. For this reason, stocks are also commonly referred to as equity or shares.

So what is a publicly listed company?

This is a company that is offering its shares to the public for the purpose of raising capital in a secondary market, referred to as the stock exchange.

So, the more stock an individual acquires from the stock market, the greater the ownership share of the company in question he or she gets, which entitles him or her to a share of the revenues of the company as well as voting rights in the company's annual general meetings.

Traditionally, a certificate of ownership of stock was issued. However, thanks to advances in technology, this is now stored electronically and held by the broker issuing the stock.

Crucially, stockowners do not have to be involved in the day-to-day running of the business. Hence, they get to own a piece of the company and its profits without actually showing up for work.

The stockowner, also referred to as the shareholder, is protected from personal liability, too. It follows that if the company goes bankrupt, the shareholder's personal assets cannot be liquidated on behalf of the company. The shareholder only loses the amount that they invested in the company.

Although many perceive the stock market as complicated and inaccessible, the way it operates is, in essence, really quite simple.

The stock exchange is one of the various ways a company raises capital for its ongoing business or expansion. Companies wishing to list their shares for trading by the public start with a process called the Initial Public Offering (IPO) where it offers its stock to the public for the very first time.

We'll see how that works shortly. Don't worry if some of the jargon is a little confusing, we'll cover everything in due course. For now, let's run over the key takeaways from this short section.

CHAPTER SUMMARY

- A stock represents ownership of a portion of a company.
- Stocks are also commonly referred to as shares or equity.
- Owners of shares are known as shareholders, stockholders or stockowners.
- A company that offers its shares / stock to the public is known as a publicly listed company.
- A shareholder has limited liability.
- If a company is profitable, the shareholders are entitled to a share of the revenues.

TYPES OF STOCKS EXPLAINED

Not all stocks, also known as shares, issued to or purchased by different shareholders are created equal. There are two main categories of shares: common and preferred. Common shares are the most popular and are often referred to as 'ordinary' shares.

COMMON SHARES

Common shares represent partial ownership of a company and, as we know, owners are entitled to a share of the company's revenues, often referred to as 'dividends'.

The amount you will earn depends on the company's figures over a specified period, ordinarily known as the 'financial year'.

Common shares also come with voting rights per share; the greater the holding, the greater the influence within the company.

Common stockholders do enjoy limited liability but, in the event of the company's liquidation, they are compensated last after preferential shareholders and other creditors.

PREFERENTIAL SHARES

Preferential stock, just like common stock, also represents a share of company ownership. The first difference between these two types of stock is in the dividend share.

Preferred stockholders receive dividends before common stockholders. Secondly, in the event of liquidation of the company's assets, preferred shareholders also get the first claim on assets before common stockholders.

Preferred stocks earn fixed dividends, which make them more of a bond or debt than an ordinary share. Consider the following analogy:

If you give someone a loan, they owe a debt to you, and you will receive fixed interests on the loan. This is the same concept as buying a bond and receiving fixed premiums, or being a preferred shareholder.

OTHER STOCK CATEGORIES

As a beginner, you will likely be dealing with common shares, but as you progress on your journey, you may come across other options such as the below:

GROWTH STOCKS

These are stocks that have potential for growth in price above the general stock market price as a benchmark. Investors who purchase these types of stocks expect continued growth in the company's earnings, hence more capital gains in the long run.

Capital gains refers to increased price of the shares, hence the investor is in a position to profit from a sale of the stocks above the purchase price.

BLUE CHIP STOCKS

These are the stocks of publicly traded industry leading companies in different sectors. These stocks tend to serve investors wishing to operate a moderately low-risk model, since they are safe and reliable, offering steady dividends. Most stockholders tend to hold onto these stocks for a long time, and many to perpetuity.

INCOME STOCKS

These stocks pay much higher dividends than other stocks. Most of them have a much lesser rate of growth than growth stocks but are attractive due to the amount of dividends they pay. These stocks also tend to serve the moderately low-risk investor.

CYCLICAL STOCKS

These stocks tend to follow the overall economy in terms of performance. For instance, in times of recession, these stocks will also fail significantly. Stocks in industries such as automotive and airlines exhibit this behavior.

DEFENSIVE STOCKS

Defensive stocks usually exhibit the opposite behavior to cyclical stocks. They do not underperform due to poor economic conditions. Companies in the food and beverage sector, for example, fit into this category of shares.

VALUE STOCKS

Value stocks are considered as underpriced by investors. These may be stocks with real earnings and potential signs of growth that come at a low price.

SPECULATIVE STOCKS

These stocks show signs of impending growth in the short-term. Investors buy these stocks in the hope of making big profits as fast as possible. They best serve high-risk investors and aren't an ideal starting place for beginners.

CHAPTER SUMMARY

- Common stocks are also known as ordinary stocks or shares, and they are the most common kind, as the name suggests. In general, when people talk about stocks, they are usually referring to these.

- Investors consider preferred stock as more of a bond or debt than an ordinary share.
- A dividend is the stockholder's share of the company's revenues or profits.

WHERE TO BUY STOCKS

Stocks are traded in exchanges. These are places where buyers and sellers of stock meet to transact their business.

Traditionally, most exchanges were physical places where trading was carried out on what was referred to as a 'trading floor'. Today, trading is also done electronically using a network of super high-speed computers.

Before exploring the different stock exchanges available, let's revisit the concept of a secondary market as mentioned previously.

Before stocks are traded on the secondary market, they have to be traded in a primary market. As discussed earlier, companies willing to list their shares for trading do so through an Initial Public Offering (IPO).

The IPO is carried out in the primary market; hence, the primary market is the stage at which shares are created. The secondary market, then, is where shares previously traded in the primary market are traded.

When referring to the stock market, in general, we usually mean the secondary market, as this is where people like us operate. You need not be too concerned with what goes on before that point, but it's useful to know.

Let's look at some of the major stock exchanges around the world.

THE NEW YORK STOCK EXCHANGE

This is the most famous stock exchange in the world, and it came into existence more than 200 years ago.

Some of the largest companies in America have their shares listed on this exchange. Most of the trading occurs on the trading floor, while orders emanate from outside brokers.

THE NASDAQ

This is a virtual exchange with no trading floor, most of the trading being done electronically through dealer communications.

This exchange also boasts some of the largest companies in America and, indeed, the world.

Another significantly large stock exchange in the United States is the American Stock Exchange (AMEX).

In London, there is the London Stock Exchange (LSE) and, in Asia, the Hong Kong Stock Exchange.

You don't need to know the ins and outs of every exchange, but it's useful to familiarize yourself with the major players. As a beginner, you may even want to monitor some of them just to get used to the practice of doing so.

CHAPTER SUMMARY

- Stocks are traded on stock exchanges.
- The secondary market of publicly listed companies is the stock market in which we operate.
- Most investing and trading is now carried out electronically.

HOW TO BUY STOCKS

As a prospective investor in the stock market, you do not necessarily have to go through the various stock exchanges to purchase shares. In fact, as a beginner, you may find some of the below options much more favorable.

You can also buy stocks through:

1. A Broker

2. DSPP/DRIP

3. Mutual Funds and ETFs

Let's take a look at the differences between these options and assess which is best for beginners.

USING A BROKER

Thanks to the emergence of new technologies, not least the prominence of the Internet in modern trading, brokers are available freely to investors, all from the comfort of their own homes.

You simply need to select the type of stock you wish to purchase depending on your expectations and risk appetite. Once a broker has this information they will provide the price-per-share and facilitate a process of payment.

Brokers, of course, charge commissions for their services, which is well worth paying since it enables you to tap directly into their professional expertise.

There are two primary types of stockbrokers available; 'regular brokers' who work directly with their clients and 'resellers' who act as intermediaries between their clients and larger brokers. Let's dive a little deeper.

REGULAR BROKERS

Regular brokers are often the preferred choice as it is easier to place your trust in someone who deals direct. The vast majority of them work with recognized organizations, making them inherently more reliable and trustworthy. Under regular brokers there are two other categories of broker, namely:

FULL-SERVICE BROKERS

These brokers work full-service, just as the name suggests, meaning that they offer more services to their clients, but at a higher cost. They will handle a lot of the legal work for you and ensure that you are well informed and advised before you make any moves.

DISCOUNT BROKERS

These brokers work part-time, therefore, much of the work is done by the investor. Investors who are new to stocks often prefer these types of brokers, as they are cheaper than their full-service counterparts.

What's more, doing much of the work yourself when you are just starting out is a great way to gain insight into how the markets work. With the Internet at your disposal, many questions can be answered without having to hire professional help.

RESELLERS

There isn't much to be said about resellers, except that they link their clients to more established brokerage service providers. Their role is limited to taking stock orders from their customers and executing the trades through larger brokers.

It is important to note that unlike major brokerages, resellers don't have to be members of any governing organizations. Therefore, they may not be as reliable as regular brokers, and you must dig deep to find one in whom you can place your trust.

CHOOSING A BROKER

When entering the markets you will need a brokerage account. As a beginner, you will be faced with a challenge when choosing the type of broker that you want to work with.

You must take great care here since different brokers are adept at handling different types of investments. You, therefore, have to be certain that the broker you choose will be able to offer you the help that you need.

Consider these aspects when selecting a broker:

TYPE OF INVESTOR

"What type of investor or trader am I?"

You must answer this question to determine the type of stockbroker to trade with. There are different types of investors and traders, as shall be explained later, and a single stockbroker cannot cater to the needs of all of them.

It is only after you define the type of investor you wish to be that you will be able to choose a broker that bests suits your needs and style of trading.

BROKERAGE FEES

The price you pay for services is an important consideration to make when you are choosing a broker to work with. Examining and comparing brokerage fees will help you avoid paying unnecessary fees on broker commissions and get a better estimate of the returns on your investments.

Some of the fees and factors you should examine before you settle on a particular broker include:

THE MINIMUMS

This is the minimum balance that is required by most brokers in order to open a brokerage account. Online discount brokers will, for instance, ask for a minimum deposit ranging between $500 and $1000.

THE MARGIN

A margin account allows you to borrow money from a broker to fulfill an investment in return for paying interest on the sum. If and when you consider trading with a margin account, you must keep in mind that the minimum balance required with this type of account is higher than that of an ordinary account.

You also have to consider the cost of trading in a margin account versus the benefits that you receive at the end of the day. The difference between the two will help you decide if a margin account is a good idea or not.

WITHDRAWAL CHARGES

Most brokers will charge a fee for making a withdrawal of money from your account. It is important that you understand all the withdrawal rules and requirements beforehand, as this will allow you to pick a broker who will help you access your money easily.

FEE STRUCTURES

The fee structures for most reputable stockbrokers are relatively similar. However, there are those who have complex fee structures that may be hard for a beginner to get to grips with. Brokerage firms that have overly complicated fee structures will usually carry some hidden charges. Therefore, it is important that you understand the fee structure intimately before you make a decision.

Other than these types of investor and brokerage fees, other factors to consider when selecting a brokerage service include its reputation and standing within the sector and the quality of information it provides.

GOING SOLO

If you were to go it alone, using the options that follow, it would be down to you to do due diligence on a company, something which requires very a particular skillset. If you were to miss one small detail, you could end up losing more than you would have paid for a broker in the first place. In any case, here are your options:

DIRECT STOCK PURCHASE PLAN (DSPP)

The second way to buy stocks is through DSPP. This approach is most commonly offered by blue chip companies to allow individual investors to buy ownership of a company directly. However, such a plan involves a lot of paperwork, which at times may require you to hire an agent or administrator to help you out.

DSPPs have minimum deposit requirements, mostly in the range of $100 to $500. It may also require a periodic investment of a specified amount, and may include a dividend reinvestment program (DRIP) whereby your dividends are put back in rather than withdrawn as cash.

MUTUAL FUNDS AND ETFS - INVESTING INDIRECTLY

Besides buying stocks through brokers or DSPP, as a beginner, you can choose to invest indirectly through mutual funds or ETFs.

MUTUAL FUNDS

Mutual funds pool money from several investors and invest it on behalf of the group. The fund may invest in stocks, bonds or other assets.

Professionals actively manage mutual funds. They pick stocks on behalf of investors, which makes this option an appealing one for new investors and traders who are preoccupied with other duties, and want to let their investments take care of themselves.

Mutual funds offer the opportunity to hold different types of stocks in companies across various industries. Most brokers have a minimum share purchase requirement, which limits how much an individual investor can diversify their portfolio.

EXCHANGE-TRADED FUNDS (ETFS)

An ETF, or Exchange-Traded Fund, owns underlying assets and splits that ownership into shares. This basket of assets tracks and trades like a regular stock. An ETF should not be mistaken for a mutual fund.

When it comes to overall liquidity, you have better options with ETFs. Also, the fees are much lower than a mutual fund, which is great if you are trading as an individual and do not want your profits to be consumed by commissions.

If you are a shareholder in an ETF or invest in a mutual fund, you do not own any shares. You cannot directly claim any of the investments in the fund. Your role is that of an indirect shareholder whose rights include dividends, profits, earned interest or residual value in the event of liquidation of the fund.

INDEX FUNDS

Index funds are a form of passive investing, since they are not actively managed. Instead, these mutual funds track the performance of a broad market such as the S&P 500. Those who invest in index funds are essentially at the mercy of the market and cannot take advantage of anomalies that allow active managers to capitalize. The upside is that this method is known to generally outperform many actively managed funds thanks to its consistency and reliability.

CHAPTER SUMMARY

- The stock market offers various means of participation, the most common being through brokerage services.
- You can also buy shares directly by going straight to the company or exchange.
- Mutual funds and ETFs offer the opportunity to spread risk and responsibility with others. They allow you to trade in stocks that you do not directly own.
- There are two main types of brokers: regular brokers and resellers. The regular brokers can either be full-service brokers or discount brokers.
- Choice of broker can be determined by brokerage fees and the type of investor or trader you wish to be.

CREATING A WINNING STRATEGY

Before you can go ahead and buy some stocks you need to create a framework for your investments. There are many things to take into consideration that will greatly influence whether or not you will be successful. These are:

GOALS

You must take time to think deeply about the ultimate purpose that drives your desire to invest in stocks. Reasons given for investing in stocks include, but are not limited to, investing for future retirement, to build an emergency fund, to make money to buy a home or other major purchase, or even to enable students to pay their college tuition.

Your reasons will guide you to the right types of stocks to invest in and the kind of trading strategy you will opt for. Come up with a written plan that clearly illustrates the value of your initial investment and your expected return on that investment after a fixed amount of time. Establish whether you have more than one investment goal and plan well for each of the goals.

This is where brokerage firms can really help out. If you are totally unsure, speak to a professional, they are often willing to provide a small amount of advice for free in order to get the wheels of your plan in motion.

TIMEFRAME

This fixed period will determine how long you will have to hold onto your stocks. For instance, if you are looking to make millions of dollars, you may have to consider a long-term investment. If you are looking for rapid results, you will gravitate towards trading strategies which yield smaller profits in shorter amounts of time.

RISK TOLERANCE

It is important to note that every single investment that you undertake has some form of risk attached to it. There is always a chance that you could lose some or all of what you put in. What level of risk are you willing to take, and how much are you willing to lose?

Only plan to invest an amount of money that you are ready to lose, just in case things don't work your way, which, at some point or another, they won't. It's also a good idea to plan for this eventuality.

TRADING OPTIONS

There is more to stocks than simply picking out shares. There are options that you can explore, and these options will allow you to manage your overall risk, as well as determine how much money you can make.

Let's look at some of the most popular ways to deal in stocks:

DAY TRADING

Stock trading is known for being intense and time-consuming, which is one of the major reasons why many beginners don't give it much thought. However, you can choose to try day trading if you are looking for quick gratification and timely returns.

As the name suggests, day trading is the practice of buying and selling a particular security in one trading day. As a trading strategy, it is best defined as short-term.

Day trading focuses around taking advantage of tiny fluctuations in the prices of stocks that are highly liquid. This strategy is also widely in the FOREX trading markets, where a small change in the value of a currency can lead to massive profits.

PENNY STOCKS

The name provides a solid indication as to what you will be dealing with here. Penny stocks are stocks trading close to a penny; $5 or less to be specific. When traded right, penny stocks can offer a decent return while helping you mitigate your risk.

A penny stock can grow as much as 300% in a day, may get even weaker, or even remain the same without significant volatility for a year. It all comes down to driving factors such as investor sentiment, the state of the market, and industry influences.

When seeking to try out stock trading without risking big losses, penny stocks are the way to get started. The amount you invest in such an equity should be based on your objectives, risk appetite, and trading aggression.

This approach requires in-depth knowledge of day trading, and serves short-term thinkers best.

DIVIDEND STOCKS

If long-term returns through stock investing motivates you, dividend stocks may be the way to go. These are the types of stocks that you purchase when you are willing to wait to get the desired returns.

Over the long run, you will find that you can accumulate a sizeable amount of wealth from returns on dividend stocks. If you choose the right company to invest in, you will also benefit from its growth and income over time.

CHAPTER SUMMARY

- Stock investing involves much more than just buying shares on the market.
- Day trading enables you to make a return within 24 hours.
- Penny stocks trading are an excellent choice if you are tentatively entering the stock trading market.
- Dividend stocks are just what you need when you are looking to grow your wealth long-term.

UNDERSTANDING STOCK ORDERS

Stock orders are essential tools in stock trading. They help a trader determine the best time to enter or exit a trading position.

An order is an instruction in the trading market to buy or sell a stock. These instructions may be sent to a broker, or be directed to the share market through market access.

Digital and Internet technologies have made it easier for both traders and investors to buy and sell stocks quickly without involving stock-brokers. Nevertheless, as a beginner, it is still important to understand orders and how to use them.

When you begin trading, you may believe that all you need to do is buy or sell in certain conditions. Though this is true, it is an incredibly simplistic way of looking at trading.

Trading requires you to be monitoring your stocks continuously and consistently to avoid losses. So, ultimately, you must be present at all times, which is not always convenient.

Orders come in handy to increase your efficiency and help you significantly minimize your risk. The best thing about using them is you do not have to be glued to the stock trading screens to ensure that you get good returns.

HOW MARKET ORDERS WORK

If you want to capitalize on the very best prices that the market has to offer, then you will make use of a market order. A market order makes it possible for you to buy or sell any stock at the best price that the market has to offer.

As a trader, there are times that you need a guarantee that your trade will be filled, and this order is the most reliable way to ensure that outcome. Should you wish to limit any possible losses that you may incur, use the market order within a market that you know has good liquidity.

You should observe the asking price as this is the point that you will fill in the market order to buy. If you want a market order to sell, then you need to fill it at the bid price. It is worth noting that the market order will not mean you have a price that is guaranteed. Instead, the fill is guaranteed.

HOW STOCK LIMIT ORDERS WORK

In the case that you value a certain price over quick execution of a trade, you should make use of a limit order. When you place a limit order, you get to buy at a particular price, or a better price, and the same applies for selling, too.

So, you can choose to put up a buy limit order or a sell limit order, which is an excellent way to manage your risk levels. However, unlike the market order, there is no guarantee of a fill.

If you don't want to deal in guesswork and blind hope, the stock limit order is the solution, as it offers you a precision guarantee. For the best results, ensure that you are on the right side of the market.

HOW TO USE STOP LOSS ORDERS

The ideal way to maintain full control of the price level on your chosen shares is to take advantage of a stop order. This order will help you to buy or sell at certain levels. If you have a limit order in place, then the stop order would work in the opposite direction.

With a buy stop order, the placement would be above the market price, and with the sell stop order, it would be below. When you have reached the stop order level, then the order is changed to a limit order or market order as per your specifications.

There are three main types of stop orders that you can use. These are the stop order, which is fairly standard, the stop limit order and the trailing stop order. While the other two stop orders are held within the marketplace, trailing stop orders are held by a broker until it is possible to complete execution.

TYPES OF ORDERS AND HOW THEY WORK

Below are the orders and their subsequent instructions:

MARKET ORDER

Buy or sell a stock at the prevailing market price.

LIMIT ORDER

Defines the maximum or minimum price to buy or sell a specified stock.

STOP ORDER

Buy or sell a stock at the prevailing market price if a specified stock price is passed.

STOP-LIMIT ORDER

If a specified price is passed, buy or sell stock at the defined maximum or minimum price.

TRAILING STOP ORDER

Buy or sell stock if the price changes unfavorably.

CHAPTER SUMMARY

- Stock orders help minimize risk and give the trader greater control of the trading experience.
- Market orders ensure that one benefits from the best possible price when buying or selling a stock.
- Limit orders help you to get the stock that you desire at a certain price.
- Stop orders will start working once you have attained a certain price level.

HOW TO READ STOCK QUOTES

A stock quote consists of several different columns, each carrying a particular detail of the company's stock.

Depending on the stock exchange or brokerage firm providing the stock quote or ticker, these columns could be arranged differently.

Facebook, Inc. Common Stock
NASDAQ: FB - Jun 17, 7:59 PM EDT

113.02 USD ↓1.37 (1.20%)
After-hours: 112.71 +0.31 (0.27%)

| 1 day | 5 day | 1 month | 3 month | 1 year | 5 year | max |

Open	114.42		Mkt cap	322.68B
High	114.43		P/E ratio	69.24
Low	112.56		Div yield	-

Google Finance - Yahoo Finance - MSN Money   Disclaimer

Let's explore some of the elements that may be included in a stock quote.

COMPANY NAME

OK, it's an obvious place to start, but companies can often trade under different names, so it's important to know who you are dealing with.

A stock quote shows the name of the company that a particular stock is listed under. This is always the company's actual name in full; the ticker is used to check the company's name in the list of traded companies in the exchange.

52 WEEK HIGH AND LOW PRICES

This is the highest and lowest price reached by a particular stock for the past 52 weeks, which equates to one year.

This gives investors the general range that a stock has been trading at so they can compare it with the current price and gauge where the market sits; in the upper range (near the high) or in the lower range (near the low).

TICKER SYMBOL

A company traded in the stock market has to have a unique symbol, normally an abbreviation of its name, to identify it. This identifier is what is referred to as the ticker symbol. The symbol makes it much easier to search for a company's securities. Examples include FB for Facebook Inc., AAPL for Apple Inc. and BABA for Alibaba Group Holdings Ltd.

DIVIDEND PER SHARE

This is not the actual monetary value of dividends paid per share, but is usually an estimated figure.

DIVIDEND YIELD

This tells you what percentage return a company pays out to its shareholders in the form of dividends. It is calculated by dividing the dividend per share by the price per share.

For example, if a company's annual dividend is $2.00 and the stock trades at $25, the dividend yield is 8% because $2.00 / $25 = 0.08.

Stock quotes that omit the dividend per share and dividend yield figures indicate that the respective companies do not pay out dividends.

TRADED VOLUME

This is the total number of shares traded for that particular trading day.

DAY'S HIGH AND LOW

Apart from the 52-week high and low, the current day's high and low are also included in some stock quotes.

CLOSE

When the stock exchange closes for business until the next day, the last price is referred to as the closing price.

CHANGE

The change from the previous day's close to the current day's close is calculated as a percentage and shown in the price quote. Mostly this is shown alongside an up or down arrow indicating a positive or negative change.

It is important to note that there are numerous stock quotes available online, each created by different stock brokers and financial companies and featuring multiple details.

Some quotes show only the current day's high, current day's low and the ticker symbol of the stock. It's up to you how deep you want to dive, but you should be well equipped to assess stocks with the information above.

CHAPTER SUMMARY

- You can now read and understand the key information contained on stock quotes. Next up, it's charts.

READING CHARTS

Stock quotes, as seen in the previous section, are a simple tabulated summary of a stock that provides information such as stock's trading price, its bid and ask price, and volume traded.

On the other hand, a stock chart provides the price data of a stock over a given period of time. This data is used to analyze the performance of the stock.

A stock chart can be presented various ways, the most common being line charts, candlestick charts and bar charts.

Let's take a look at the differences between each:

LINE CHARTS

Many charting platforms offered by stockbrokers use this method. It does not show the highs and lows for each particular day, week or month.

Line charts only show the closing prices of a particular stock represented as a line of the close-to-close prices.

Reading them is simple; just find the date on the horizontal axis

directly below any point

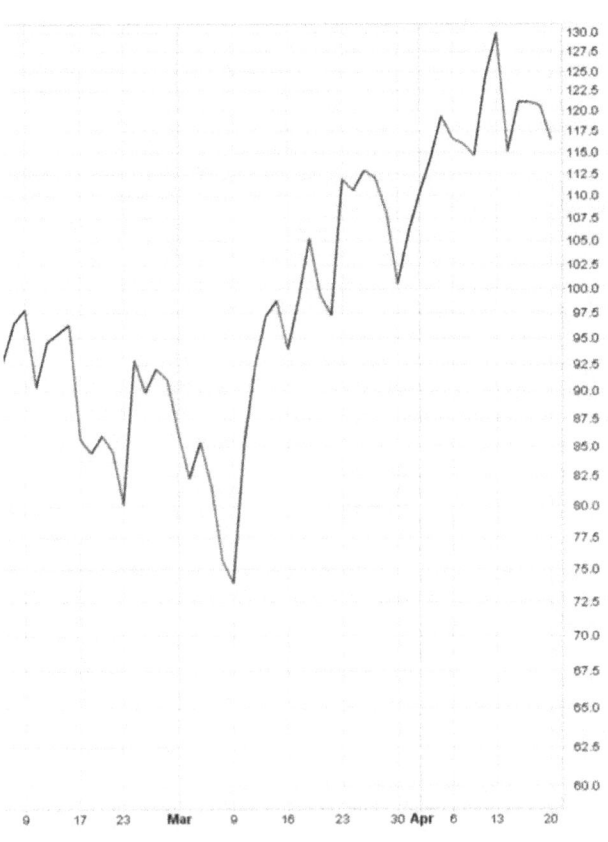

to find the closing price for that day. Check out the below example.

BAR CHARTS

A bar chart shows the opening, closing, high and low price for each day represented by bars.

To read it, simply use the same method as you did for the line graph, matching individual points to the particular date that you require information for.

CANDLESTICK CHARTS

This has the same features as the bar chart but it's easier to view as its body is larger, showing the open, high, low and close more vividly.

This is the most common charting method that is used today. To read it, use the very same method that you've already learnt.

Give it a go with the below example and enjoy that surge of satisfaction that comes with understanding the simplicity of something which used to seem so complicated!

A Note on Stock Price Gaps

Sometimes when you are analyzing your chart, you may notice something strange - a period during which the price of a chosen stock experiences a sharp movement, whether it be up or down. Within this movement, there will be minimal or no trading that has occurred. This period is an indication that there is a gap between the chosen prices.

There are various reasons that a gap may show up in your chart, with one popular reason being a merger that may have affected the security of your stock. A good investor will analyze what is happening within the gap, especially the cost of the stock, and see how it is possible to capitalize on it for the purpose of profit.

There are four types of gaps, namely:

• **Breakaway gap**

• **Common gap**

• **Runaway gap**

• **Exhaustion gap**

To differentiate between the gaps, you will find that a common gap is quite small. When a business is going through a period of consolidation, it is common to see a breakaway gap that is wider than the common gap. This is the type of gap that will let you know when a trend is starting.

If there is a strong move in price, you will see the runaway gap, and it will appear close to the center of a trend. It reveals that the intensity of the trend is increasing.

The exhaustion gap is seen at the end of the trend, and it is not a good sign. You will see this gap when the trend is getting ready to reverse, revealing a weakness in the market.

Higher Highs On A Stock Chart

Once you begin going through stock charts more regularly, the numbers will begin to speak to you in a way that you can understand, like a language. Within that language, one of the aspects that you will look out for is the higher high.

This is an indicator that lets you know that you need to start buying your preferred stock. You will see a higher high when there is movement in the stock. This movement could show that the price retracts from a previous high point that was temporary for weeks, and then moves above this previous high and closes.

It could also be an indication that the stock has found technical resistance, and when it is above this resistance, you must buy, and when it falls below it, you must sell.

For the best higher highs, look for an uptrend in the market. You could also choose a stock that is in an industry that is hot at the time.

CHAPTER SUMMARY

- You can read the stock market prices using a stock quote or stock chart.
- The main charting methods include the line chart, bar chart and candlestick chart.
- Different brokers and financial authorities use different quoting and charting platforms.
- Not all stock quotes and charts have the same standard features as described above; some have fewer features while others provide more information.

WHY STOCK PRICES CHANGE

Market forces are the drivers of stock prices. Just like any other commodity, prices are determined by demand and supply.

DEMAND

The higher the demand for a stock, the higher the share price. If there are more buyers than sellers, prices will tend to rise.

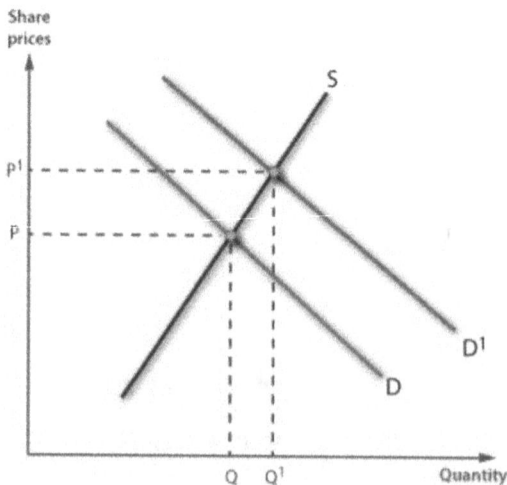

Factors That Influence Demand

Below are some company fundamentals that will change investors' thoughts towards the value of a company's stock, and hence its demand.

Earnings per Share

Companies with sustained growth in their earnings tend to be more valuable to investors. These companies invest a significant amount of their revenues back into business growth.

Companies with high earnings have enough to pay dividends to their shareholders as well as reinvest in the growth of the company, making them a formidable long-term prospect.

Price : Earnings Ratio

Companies with a lower price earnings ratio compared to other companies in the industry are seen as more valuable to investors.

The price earnings ratio is calculated by dividing the price of the stock by its earnings per share for the last twelve months.

For example, if the earnings were $1.5 and the stock price is $25, the P:E would be $(25/1.5) = 16.67$.

This effectively measures how much in monetary terms investors are willing to pay for each dollar earning of the company.

Dividend Yield

Increasing dividends give investors extra income to reinvest in the stock market. Hence, companies that offer higher dividends are considered valuable by investors.

However, if dividends are lowered so as to increase investment in the company's operations or retire debt capital, it may be seen as a shrewd long-term move by the company and hence increase investors' demand for the stock.

As with many things in the world of stocks, your own priorities and goals will determine your perception of value.

Book Value

Investors look at the book value of a company in comparison with its peers in the industry. This value is the difference between the company's liabilities and assets. Liabilities are inclusive of preferred stock issued by the company.

The figure is measured against each share (book value per share). If the company's stock price is below book value, that stock is cheap. For a stock to have higher value while cheap, it must show potential for improvement, otherwise it is considered unpromising.

Return on Equity

ROE shows how efficient a company is at generating a profit from each unit of shareholder equity. A company is considered valuable if its returns on equity are higher than those of its peers in the same industry.

Supply

The higher the supply, the lower the stock price. If there are more sellers than buyers, prices will tend to fall. It follows that stocks that are in high demand from investors will tend to increase in value more than stocks that do not have such demand.

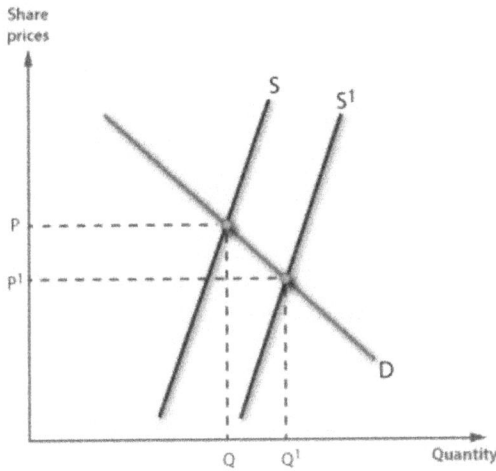

SHORT SELLING

Investors will sell stocks that they hold if they believe they no longer hold value, pushing their prices down. Prices can also be affected by a practice called short selling.

Short selling is when investors borrow stocks not owned and sell them in the market at the current price with the hope of buying them back later at a lower price.

It's not necessary to go into detail on such techniques right now; suffice it to say this is just another way that valuations can fluctuate.

Ultimately the value of a stock comes down to what investors feel a company is worth. Investors look at various things, for instance, assets and management to value a business.

This value is not only the current value of the company; it also represents how much an investor thinks a company will be worth in the future given its growth and other macroeconomic factors.

CHAPTER SUMMARY

- Stock prices change due to market forces of demand and supply.
- Investors' perceptions influence demand for a company's stock.
- High demand for a company's stock will cause its price to go up while higher supply than demand will lead to the fall of the stock's price.
- Investors should look at a company's fundamental data to assess its value and hence the value of its stock.

SMART STOCK SELECTION

The first thing to ask yourself before purchasing a company's stock is: 'What kind of investment am I making?'

There are different market cycles, and every investor may have different long-term and short-term goals when investing in the stock market.

Each investor's financial situation at the time of investing in the stock market is also different. Similarly, as discussed previously, investors should analyze various fundamental factors about a company before buying its stock.

Investors who do not use advised methods such as brokers or mutual funds for purchasing stocks will have to make their own decisions on which stocks to buy.

There are two main methods that investors use to make purchasing decisions. One is fundamental analysis, and the other is technical analysis. Let's see what each method entails.

FUNDAMENTAL ANALYSIS

This method uses freely available company data or information to estimate the value of an individual stock. It focuses on current factors as well as the future growth potential of a company.

Fundamental analysis takes into account the geographical location of the company and the overall economic situation of that region. Generally speaking, regions with high economic growth potential have a positive effect on the companies located in those regions.

Apart from the geographical region, fundamental analysis also narrows down to the industry in which the company operates. It further compares the company with its peers in that same industry.

In simple terms, fundamental analysis focuses on issues that affect the company both internally and externally. Most of the data discussed in the previous chapter is used when making a decision on whether to buy the company's stock or not.

TECHNICAL ANALYSIS

This form of analysis attempts to predict the future price or trend of stock by analyzing past historical price charts.

We've already looked at line, bar and candlestick charts. These are analyzed to predict the future value of stock.

Technical analysts believe that all fundamental data is already shown in the stock chart and hence try to establish certain profitable patterns and trends on the charts.

Some of the techniques used can be quite advanced, and how far down the rabbit hole you go will depend on your own objectives.

The two methods discussed above fit different investors while some utilize both. The main thing to consider is risk appetite, which dictates the types of stocks to buy as discussed in chapter two.

Similarly, research and knowledge, such as the information offered in this guide, are important so that investors can clearly understand the type of investment they are undertaking.

Investing in reliable price feeds and charting platforms, especially for technical analysts, also forms part of a successful investment in the stock market.

Finally, we can break down stock market investors into the following categories based on their risk appetite and financial expectations:

VALUE INVESTORS

These people look to buy stocks that are underpriced and have a high potential to increase in value leading to high capital gains.

GROWTH INVESTORS

These folk buy stocks belonging to companies that have innovative products that show the capability of being market leaders or dominating their particular industry.

INCOME INVESTORS

These are people looking for recurrent and steady returns in terms of dividends. They buy into companies that show historically robust dividend payouts and a will to reward shareholders.

TRADERS

These guys look for various trends in the market and create their bias based on historical price patterns and data, seeking to profit from speculating in the stock market over a short-to-medium-term period. We'll learn more about traders in the next chapter.

CHAPTER SUMMARY

- There are two primary methods that investors use to decide which stocks to buy; fundamental and technical analysis.
- Those who do not wish to make their own investment decisions can use advisory services such as brokers or mutual funds.
- A decision on which stocks to buy is also based on an investor's risk tolerance and financial expectations.

TRADING VS INVESTING

In the world of stocks, one is either an investor or a trader. Let's explore what each side entails to create a clear distinction.

TRADERS

Individuals who would like to make as much money as possible in the shortest time frame are called traders. The timeframe for their investments normally ranges from a few minutes to a few weeks.

Traders have a higher appetite for risk and a short-term perspective of the markets; they have a get-in get-out mentality.

There is always a significant possibility that you will make profits as a trader, but to do so, you will first have to determine the kind of trader you want to be. There are numerous types of traders out there, and the one you choose to be will depend on your personality, your capital investment and the amount of time that you can dedicate to trading.

Here are the most popular types of traders in the stock market today:

SWING TRADERS

These are considered as the most efficient types of stock traders. These types of traders will base their trades on a longer time frame, then sit back and watch stocks for weeks or even months before they make a trading decision.

They follow the momentum of the market when they are buying or selling stocks, explaining their name. When the stock prices start going up, swing traders will buy whatever stocks they have their eyes on and when the prices get to a point where they feel they have reached their peak, they sell their position rapidly.

You have to be remarkably smart if you would like to be this type of a trader, as in-depth knowledge of fundamental and technical analysis is necessary. A swing trader does not need to be on the lookout the entire day, therefore, if you would like to make some money as a stock trader, but do not have enough time to dedicate entire days to the practice, this is a solid option for you.

VALUE TRADERS

This is the kind of trader who invests in undervalued stocks that are selling below their inherent value. For instance, if the stock of a company has been affected by various market conditions and its value drops significantly, a diligent value trader will invest in those stocks in the hope that things will get better in the future, and there will be a chance for them to make a profit. They will then sell when they feel the price has reached a more reasonable level.

BUY AND HOLD TRADERS

These are the kind of traders who will buy stocks and hold them for an extended period until they feel that the right time to sell has come. They can even hold the stocks for decades. In most cases, these types of traders are interested in stocks of well-established companies because there is a high chance that they will make some good money out of their investment.

DAY TRADERS

These folk hold and exit many trading positions within one trading day. They are also known as scalpers or intra-day traders. These are the kinds of traders who expose themselves to high trading risks with the knowledge that they will get high returns if their investments turn out in their favor, making this a very attractive proposition for the masses.

Day traders buy and hold positions for as little as a few seconds before they sell. They work full-time and have to be on the lookout every minute and every second until the trade closes. This, then, is a great way to make rapid income, but not passive income.

INVESTORS

On the other side of the coin we have investors. Think of them as snipers waiting to take the right shot. They pick a stock that they think will increase in value, then buy and hold it.

For example, someone who bought Coca-Cola stock several years ago and now has a few million shares worth would be an investor.

Do you think that Facebook (NASDAQ: FB) will completely take over the social media scene? Will Google (NASDAQ: GOOG) dominate the information scene for years to come? If you decide to buy stocks and for whatever reason hold onto them for the long-term you are an investor.

Just as there are different types of stocks to invest in, there are also different types of stock investors. No choice is inherently better than the other; you must choose the type of investor you want to become depending on your trading personality.

Here are the different types of investors within the stock market:

ACTIVE INVESTORS

This is the kind of investor who undertakes investing as both a business and a passion. They will read everything there is to know about investing, join associations, subscribe to magazines and newsletters and dive deep into their research.

They are full-time investors who ordinarily have no other form of income. They take their investments very seriously and will invest in any stock that they feel will bring returns. They pick their stocks wisely, depending on the state of the market, the stock price behaviors and also the earnings growth, meaning they are unlikely to succumb to mistakes.

PASSIVE INVESTORS

These are the kinds of investors who wish to invest their money in the stock market but do not have time to do the legwork. Passive investors normally partner with a full-time broker because they do not have enough time to study the market.

All they are interested in is a return on their investment and not all the work that goes on behind the scenes. Sometimes passive investors may even place their money in stocks on a whim, essentially gambling that they will be able to pull some profits later down the line.

BARGAIN HUNTER INVESTORS

These investors step in and save failing companies with cash injections. If they believe a company has the potential to flourish in future, they will put up capital in return for stock and reap the rewards later down the line. Returns can be massive, but not every story has a fairytale ending.

CHAPTER SUMMARY

- Stock traders engage in trading of equities for profit. They include day, buy and hold, swing and value traders.
- Stock investors use their money to buy stocks with growth potential for returns in the form of interest, capital gains or dividends.
- Different types of investors are not mutually exclusive; you

can practice any of the strategies depending on your availability, plan, and goals.

- When investing, you need to picture yourself as a part owner of the company whose stock you are buying. As a trader, you need to look for short-term profit opportunities – you're just keeping those shares warm!

STOCK MARKET JARGON EXPLAINED

As you embark on your trading or investing journey, you will stumble across so much jargon that it will feel like you are learning a different language at times.

Some stuff is superfluous, while other sayings are part of the very fabric of the markets. Here's a quick run-down of some of the most common stock market sayings:

BULLS AND BEARS

Investors who are looking to sell stocks are called 'bears,' while those looking to buy are called 'bulls.

BULL MARKET

When the environment in the economy is great: healthy employment, improved Gross Domestic Product, stock market performing well, etc.

BEAR MARKET

The opposite of a bull market; when the market takes a dip due to a recession in the economy or other external factors.

STOCK CODE

The stock symbol (mostly comprised of the company's initials) that is assigned to each stock.

MARKET PRICE

This is the current price per share of stock during its trading hours.

BID PRICE

The price at which buyers are willing to buy a stock.

BID SIZE

The total number of shares that buyers are willing to buy at the current bid price.

ASK PRICE

The price at which sellers are willing to sell stock.

ASK SIZE

The total number of shares that sellers are willing to sell at the current ask price.

TICK SIZE

The smallest price movement of stock.

LOT SIZE

The standard position size of the trade in stocks that stockbrokers allow traders to operate within. As an analogy, if you are buying cooking oil, the standard size is 1 liter, but you can also buy 10 liters, 3 liters or even half a liter. Similarly, stocks have a standard size, and you can buy several lots or even a fraction of a lot.

PRIMARY MARKET

A market where new shares are traded.

SECONDARY MARKET

The market where existing or shares already issued trade.

LONG POSITION

A buying position in the market.

SHORT POSITION

A selling position in the market.

SHORT SELLING

Sale of shares that one does not already own by borrowing in the hope of buying them at a lower price in future.

STOP LOSS

An order for the stockbroker to close a particular position at a loss when the loss reaches a certain threshold.

TAKE PROFIT - An order to the broker to close a position in profit when the profit reaches a certain threshold.

AVERAGING DOWN

When an investor decides to invest more money in a stock whose price is going down. In the end, your average buying price will be low.

BETA

The capacity that is used to determine the price of a stock against the change experienced in the entire stock market. If a particular stock, for instance, has a beta of 1.3, it means that for every movement in the stock exchange, the stock moves 3 points or the other way round.

BLUE CHIP STOCKS

Stocks of leading companies in the industry. They are the large, well-established companies that pay better dividends consistently, and they are well known for stable management, making them the best choice for many investors who want to invest their money where there is a the best chance of returns.

BROKER

A person or entity that will buy or sell shares on your behalf and charge you a small amount of money for it, as commission.

DIVIDEND

Part of a company's income paid to its shareholders after a specified period, usually done on a quarterly or yearly basis. However, not all companies pay dividends.

PORTFOLIO

A collection of stocks that an investor owns in different companies. You can invest in just one stock, or as many as you like. Your portfolio holds them all.

SPREAD

The difference between the bid and the asking price of stock or the amount of money that an investor is willing to pay for a specified stock against the value that someone else is prepared to sell at.

CHAPTER SUMMARY

- You will come across these terms, and many others, during your trading or investing journey. Keep this guide handy to refer back to so you can keep things moving.

TIPS FOR LONG-TERM SUCCESS

Choosing to be a long-term investor may seem daunting, or even unexciting compared to the more immediate gratification of short-term strategies. However, the potential for success is massive, if you follow certain guidelines.

Here are some important tips that can help you attain success as a long-term investor:

KEEP THE WINNERS AND SELL THE LOSERS

As an investor, you will hold onto stocks hoping that their prices will go up in future, however, you must realize that there is always a limit. If there is no chance that the stock price will go up, you should sell immediately to avoid losing more in the future.

You always have to know when to let go of the stocks that are losing their value, and for many stocks, this should be immediate to avoid losing all of your investment in the long run.

Many investors would greatly benefit if they learned how to hold onto stocks worth holding onto, those whose prices seems promising in the future, and sell the stocks that have no hope of turning a profit.

THERE IS NO SUCH THING AS A HOT TIP

You will have numerous people coming to you with all manner of tips and strategies that may seem great at the time, but you have to stick to your trading style and plan if you do not want to make costly mistakes.

You should always have a good reason for making certain investments, and these reasons should always begin with thorough research before you finally decide to invest. If anyone comes to you with an idea that seems promising, take your time to think about it, instead of rushing to invest your money in it.

IGNORE THE SMALL THINGS

As a long-term investor, a slight change in a stock price should not bother you at all. Always remember that you have time to enjoy a significant shift in the stock price. If, for instance, you invest in a stock and its price goes down almost immediately, this should not bother you at all.

Look at the bigger picture; as long as you have invested in high-quality stocks, there is always a chance that they will give you good returns in the future. As such, small matters should not affect your decision to invest in a stock if you had already set your mind to do so.

STICK TO THE STRATEGY

Establish a strategy based on solid research and stick to it. One mistake many new investors make is to jump from one trading strategy to the other. Inconsistency is the reason why many investors are not enjoying favorable returns from their stock investments. There are so many trading strategies to choose from, and the one that you pick should be determined by your investment goals and your personality as a trader.

FOCUS ON THE LONG-TERM

Many new investors are lured to get rich quick schemes by the prospect of short-term returns, which is why it is becoming increasingly difficult to start off as a long-term investor.

However, if you wish to build a life around your stocks portfolio, long-term investing is the way to go. If this is what you would like to achieve, you have to forget about 'get in, get out' strategies.

One of the main benefits you enjoy here is that long-term investors do not experience the risks involved in short-term trading. So as a long-term investor, you have a higher chance of making significant returns in the long run.

KEEP AN OPEN MIND

This is one of the most important things to consider when you become an investor. Some companies, for instance, may have a great name in their respective industries, but this does not mean that they are doing well and benefiting their investors.

You will come to realize that there are many small companies that offer greater returns than some of the most popular companies on the market. You, therefore, have to keep an open mind and go for exactly what you are looking for, even if that means ignoring the major players.

KEEP EMOTIONS AT BAY

Investments do not work well if emotions are allowed into play. Separating your emotions from your objectives will make it easier for you to make sound investment decisions, but if you allow your emotions to cloud your judgment, you may fall into the trap that many stock investors find themselves in.

So as to do the right thing, as far as making investment decisions is concerned, you have to keep your mind open, without getting attached to any stocks. For example, if an investment fails, don't look at others like they too will fail; learn to separate everything and you will always get over any failure in readiness to celebrate success.

DIVERSIFY

If you want to enjoy an easier journey, do not be the kind of investor who ties himself to just one type of stock because if that stock starts failing, so will the rest.

The advantage of diversifying is that you give yourself a chance to enjoy the various benefits that different companies have to offer to their investors. If one investment fails and the others are doing well, you may not lose any money in the end because the returns from the other investments will cover the one that is failing.

Invest a small amount of money in different companies and different industries, and you will always enjoy returns from your investments.

QUICK START GUIDE

So, we've taken a look at how to succeed long-term, but of course that will only be possible if you take a leap and get started now.

Some people start out in stocks with barely any capital, and do very well thanks to smart and successful investments. It all comes down to strategy.

As you have already learned in the previous chapters, the stock market is very complex, so start small and choose your investment strategies wisely. Here are some key tips to getting started:

START NOW

You need to know that the longer you invest in an individual stock, the more your investment is likely to produce favorable returns.

So, it is advisable to start investing as soon as you feel the urge to do so. Give your investment time to reward you and you will not be disappointed. Postponing an investment will never yield results for you, so do not take too much time before pulling the trigger.

CREATE YOUR PLAN

This cannot be emphasized enough. If you want to succeed in stocks, you need to start with a plan. You need to plan for the amount of money you will spend and how you will be trading in stocks to realize a certain amount in returns.

The plan should act as a guide to help you make the right decisions at all times, so as to get exactly what you designed to at the end of a given period. Achieving your investment goals becomes very easy when you start with a sound plan.

Use the advice contained in this guide to decide which kind of trader or investor you want to be, then set about planning your budget and target industries.

SEPARATE INVESTMENTS FROM CASH RESERVES

Since it is very easy to get emotionally attached to stock investing to a point of spending all the money that you have, including your cash reserves, you need to split the two apart.

Spending all the money you have is a big risk because the time will come that you need some back and you might be forced to sell off some of your stocks at a lower price, essentially making a loss.

Besides, think of what would happen if you invested in stocks that turned out not to be as promising as you thought. You may end up losing everything you put in. So, set aside some money for stock investment and spend only that money. You can then put away more money with time when you are sure that the other investments are doing well.

INVEST WITH EXPERTISE

When starting out it's a good idea to buy stocks in businesses that you understand, rather than those that you simply like the look of.

In fact, this should be the first step you take before you even think of putting your money in a company's stock. You have to know how the business operates, the state of its financial records, its creditors and debtors, its future plans and anything else that will help you make the right decision in the end.

It is very easy to be swayed if you do not understand a business, and you could end up regretting it. For that reason, if you already hold expertise in some particular area, that would be a good place to start.

CHAPTER SUMMARY

- There is no particular formula for avoiding the downs in the financial roller-coaster ride, but with a smart strategy you can maximize your returns while minimizing risk.
- In a nutshell, to be a shrewd stock investor, you must be an excellent researcher and planner, be quick in your decisions, and have an open mind devoid of emotions.

CONCLUSION

Many people will never be enlightened to the opportunities that exist within the stock market. By reading this book, you are already one step ahead of the pack.

Are you ready to become an investor in the stock market? Or are you prepared to make your first trade? Whichever route you choose to go down the knowledge you have acquired here will serve you well along the way.

By reading the information contained in this guide, you are already invested in the stock market. You are now in a position to improve your financial life by establishing control and taking action.

THINGS TO REMEMBER

- You know how the stock market operates, so you can choose the right medium to invest through depending on your risk tolerance and financial expectations.
- You know that by purchasing shares of a particular company you are buying a slice of that business, so invest where you see potential.

- Take caution and invest only capital you are prepared to lose.
- Review the different types of stocks available and choose those that suit your investment goals.

TAKING A LEAP

Making your first move can seem like an intimidating prospect, but it need not be. Here are some final words of reassurance to get you on your way:

- You do not require a lot of capital to get started in stocks compared to other forms of investment, for instance, property or real estate.
- Dealing in stocks allows fast liquidation; you can sell your stocks quickly if needs be.
- Upkeep requires minimal time input meaning you can effectively make money while you sleep.
- The stock market is intuitive to learn as you go along.
- Your first move needn't be a big one; there are plenty of smaller opportunities out there allowing you to earn while you learn.

Ultimately, the next step is yours to take. You now have a solid foundation in place, and a resource to refer back to at any time.